TEACHER

TUNE-UPS

Donna Clark Goodrich

RadiantBOOKS
Gospel Publishing House/Springfield, Mo. 65802

02-0754

Every effort has been made to trace copyright holders—without results in a few instances. This will be rectified in future editions if the relevant information can be obtained.

Unless otherwise indicated, all Scripture quotations are taken from the HOLY BIBLE: NEW INTERNATIONAL VERSION. Copyright © 1978 by the New York International Bible Society. Used by permission of Zondervan Bible Publishers.

© 1984 by the Gospel Publishing House, Springfield, Missouri 65802. All rights reserved. No part of this book may be reproduced, stored in a retrieval system, or transmitted in any form or by any means—electronic, mechanical, photocopy, recording, or otherwise—without prior written permission of the copyright owner, except brief quotations used in connection with reviews in magazines or newspapers.

Library of Congress Catalog Card Number 84-80655
International Standard Book Number 0-88243-754-2
Printed in the United States of America

To
Clara Mae Bostwick,
my Sunday school teacher as
a teenager,
who early taught me
that
"To have a friend you must be one"
and that
"A person can have just as much of God as
he wants"

Contents

1. Individuals Are Important   9
2. The One-Note Singer   10
3. Loving Is of God   11
4. Holes in the Fences   13
5. Sowing the Seed   14
6. Don't Excuse It—Confess It!   15
7. 20-20 Vision   16
8. The Other Side of the Fence   17
9. Prayer—The Groundwork   19
10. Faith To Move Classes   20
11. Are We Responsible?   21
12. Looking Beyond the Obvious   22
13. Marked by Love   24
14. Win Them One by One   25
15. Involved in the Body   26
16. Our Investment   28
17. Are We Qualified?   29
18. With Many Parables   31

19. Leading the Leader 32
20. Never Alone 33
21. More Than We Can Imagine 35
22. Only a Boy 36
23. Loving the Unlovely 37
24. Go Out 38
25. Sharing Your Life 39
26. Study To Be Approved 40
27. A Cry of Prayer 42
28. The Day of Small Things 43
29. "He Puts the Waddle in the Duck" 44
30. Doers—Not Just Hearers 46
31. Let the Children Come 47
32. The Teacher as Evangelist 48
33. Laborers With God 50
34. The Personal Touch 51
35. Diamonds in the Rough 52

36. Time To Teach 53
37. The Comforter Is Come 55
38. Where Is the Oboe? 56
39. Welcome Home, Children 57
40. Who Cares? 58
41. Bands of Love 59
42. A Better Teacher 61
43. Pedestrian Grace 62
44. A Show of Faith 63
45. The Hardening of Sin 65
46. To the Unknown Teacher 66
47. Little Is Much 67
48. The Faithful Shepherd 69
49. One Day at a Time 70
50. "Take Care of My Sheep" 71
51. God's Instrument 72
52. The Way 74

1
Individuals Are Important

"I tell you that in the same way there is more rejoicing in heaven over one sinner who repents than over ninety-nine righteous persons who do not need to repent" (Luke 15:7).

Jesus was interested in individuals. Some of His greatest truths were presented to just one person. When Nicodemus came to Him at night, Christ didn't invite him to come to the synagogue the next Sabbath; He met his need right then.

Individuals are important! *You cannot have compassion for the multitude without first having concern for the individual.*

The entire fifteenth chapter of Luke deals with the importance of the individual: the parable of the lost sheep, the lost coin, and the lost son.

Let us notice three things about the sheep, the coin, and the prodigal son—three things for encouraging our appreciation of each of our students' value to God:

1. Someone was aware of the loss
2. Someone did something about it
3. Someone rejoiced when the lost was found

Individuals were important to Jesus. He took time for them (Nicodemus, the woman at the well, Zacchaeus). Are individuals also important to us?

Lord, help us to see our class not just as a group, but as individuals. Help us to be aware of any loss and do something about it that we may know the rejoicing of heaven over one who is found. Amen.

2

The One-Note Singer

"Through the grace of God we have different gifts. If our gift is . . . teaching let us give all we have to our teaching" (Romans 12:6,7, *Phillips*).

There once was a tenor singer in California, Myron Niesley, who was called the highest-paid radio singer because he received an enormous sum for singing *one note*—the final and top one of a theme song, which others in the chorus could not hit so perfectly.[1]

God has unique purposes for each of us. One of life's highest satisfactions comes with learning to cooperate with those purposes.

Toil-worn I stood and said,
"O Lord, my feet have bled,
My hands are sore,
I weep, my efforts vainly poor.
With fainting heart I pray of Thee,
Give some brave other, work designed for me."

But my Lord answer made,
"O child of Mine,
I have looked through space and searched

through time,
There is none can do the work called thine."

Soul-sick I knelt and cried,
"Let me forever hide
My little soul
From sight of Him who made me whole,
My one small spirit in the vast,
Vast throngs of like mean myriads, present, past!"

But my Lord answer made,
"O child of Mine,
I have looked through space and searched
    through time,
But I find no soul is like to thine!"

—Frances Bent Dillingham

Whatever the size or composition of your class, measure your significance as a teacher by whether you are where God wants you to be, doing what God wants you to do.

Lord, You have chosen us and You have given us a place in which You would have us serve. Help us to be faithful. Amen.

3

Loving Is of God

"Since God so loved us, we also ought to love one another" (1 John 4:11).

If anyone should be an expert in the art of loving it is a Sunday school teacher. He may not use the latest classroom aids. He may not be particularly fluent in teaching the lesson. But such deficiencies the student will overlook if the teacher shows love.

The teacher's love will reach out to all the students. Love sees past the physical appearance, past the family background, past the unruly behavior. Love sees an individual to be loved, accepted, and taught.

Love changes the one being loved as well as the one who is loving. Do you find yourself getting irritated with a certain student in your class? As soon as the class is over, do you begin griping about something he did that bothered you? Are you just a little relieved when he is absent? Try loving him a little more. Maybe he won't change, but *you* will.

Perhaps we are too busy to love. We don't have time to get involved. In *The Christian's Secret of a Happy Life,* Hannah Whitall Smith makes this observation: "We never care about the little details of people's lives unless we love them. . . . As soon as we begin to love anyone, we begin at once to care."[2]

How much do we know about our students? If we love, if we care, if we are really concerned, we will want to know them.

Lord, You loved us before we loved You. You loved us when we were unlovable. You looked past what we were to what we could become through Your love. Give us the ability to see what our students can become—through Your love and ours. Amen.

4
Holes in the Fences

"The younger son . . . set off for a distant country" (Luke 15:13).

A father took his son on his knee and told him the story of a lost sheep: how it found a hole in the fence and crawled through, how it wandered so far that it could not find its way back home. And then he told of the wolf that chased the sheep, and how finally the shepherd came and rescued it and carried it back to the fold. The little boy was greatly interested, and when the story was over, he asked, "Did they nail up the hole in the fence?"[3]

The Bible never tells us why the Prodigal Son left home. It does not say if there was a generation gap between the son and father. The mother is never mentioned. We might guess, from the older brother's attitude upon the prodigal son's return, that there was jealousy and competition between the brothers.

So, too, we may never know why a student leaves the classroom one Sunday and never returns. But it may be that we need to nail up the holes in our classroom fences. To spend more time in lesson preparation, in follow-up, and in prayer.

We can't wait until our students leave. We must try to keep them from straying in the first place. We mustn't worry so much about getting an ambulance to them once they have fallen over the cliff, but should put a rail at the top to keep them from going over.

Lord, if there is someone in our class who has been

gone several Sundays, help us to find out the reason why, and then help us to mend the hole in the fence before others get out. Amen.

5

Sowing the Seed

"I planted the seed, Apollos watered it, but God made it grow" (1 Corinthians 3:6).

On the way home from church one Sunday morning, a seven-year-old girl asked her mother what it meant to have a "star in your crown." The mother explained that some people believe a Christian will receive a star in his crown for each person he has led to the Lord.

Whether or not this idea is true, we do know God wants us to tell others about Jesus. The Sunday school class is an ideal setting for explaining the way of salvation to our students. Sometimes, however, we use religious terms that may be foreign to some students. Allowing time for discussion and feedback from the students may help clarify the salvation message for those who want to share it as well as for those who may be hearing it for the first time. Sensitivity to the leading of the Holy Spirit and to the needs of the students is crucial.

We must remember that even though we share Christ with a student we may not necessarily be the one to actually "say the sinner's prayer" with him. We may sow the seed, another may water it, and someone else may reap the harvest. The sower and reaper are co-workers, but "God . . . makes things grow" (1 Corinthians 3:7).

Lord, heighten our sensitivity to Your Spirit and increase our humility as before You we present Your wonderful plan of salvation to our students. Amen.

6
Don't Excuse It—Confess It!

"They all alike began to make excuses" (Luke 14:18).

A minister tells of the time he and a friend were returning from a college board meeting and noticed some police officers getting on the train with eighteen convicts in handcuffs. The minister introduced himself and asked if he might speak to the men and find out how they had become criminals.

The first prisoner didn't want to talk, but the second was very friendly. This man, who was awaiting his day of execution, told the minister he had attended Sunday school as a child. He even showed the minister a New Testament his teacher had given him.

The minister asked why he had dropped out of Sunday school. The prisoner didn't know for sure. "Did a Sunday school teacher come to invite you back?" the minister inquired. "Not that I recall," was the reply. Then the prisoner looked out the window and said, "If I hadn't dropped out of Sunday school, how differently my life might have ended."[4]

Students have many excuses for not coming to church. But excuse-making didn't begin with them. "I have bought a piece of ground, and I must needs go and see it. . . .

I have bought five yoke of oxen, and I go to prove them. . . . I have married a wife, and therefore I cannot come" (Luke 14:18-20). Excuse-making is a human failing. And a teacher can be as guilty as the next person. But God would rather have an honest confession than an excuse. Then He has something to work with.

Lord, we are too quick to make excuses. Teach us to acknowledge our failings and then confess them to You. Only then will we be able to leave our excuse-making behind.

7
20-20 Vision

"Jesus looked hard at him and said, 'You are Simon son of John; you are to be called Cephas'—meaning Rock" (John 1:42, *The Jerusalem Bible*).

Robert Troutman in his book *Better Senior High Teaching* gives the following suggestions as qualifications for a teacher:
 emotional maturity
 patience
 a youthful spirit
 a vision that something really worthwhile
  can be accomplished with the group
 flexibility
 imagination
 a sense of humor

willingness to train oneself to be a better worker
ability to listen
ability to organize[5]

Probably none of us has all these qualifications, but we should possess at least two: the vision and the willingness to train ourselves.

Mr. Troutman goes on to say, "God will help us develop these qualifications. Effective workers do not just happen. They are trained. Some may have more natural talent than others, but any person who has the interest and vision can become an effective teacher."[6]

As one Sunday school teacher expressed it: The teacher who would be successful, as the Lord counts success, must have vision. He must see people first as they are—in all their need, with all their conflicts, wrestling with perplexities and temptations. But he must have a greater vision. He must see them not only as they are now, but also as they will be when God is finished with them. Such a vision is necessary for the Lord's sake, the church's sake, and the student's sake.

Lord, give us this vision. As You saw beyond us to what we could be, help us to see what You can do with these pupils. Don't let us give up on them. You didn't give up on us. Amen.

8
The Other Side of the Fence

"Let us not be weary in doing good, for at the proper time we will reap . . . if we do not give up" (Galatians 6:9).

There is probably no job as rewarding, yet at the same time as discouraging, as being a Sunday school teacher. A new student looks promising, then for no apparent reason, drops out. Another may not grow spiritually in the measure we think he should.

This is a day of being in a hurry and wanting quick results—a day of instant cake mix, instant oatmeal, instant soup. Sometimes we also want instant success in our Sunday school work, failing to realize that real success takes time.

What would we think of a farmer who planted a field of corn, then after two or three weeks plowed up the field in discouragement because the corn was not ready to pick? God needs time to work out His purposes.

We must remember that we may reap the fruit from the seed sowed years before by another teacher, and the seeds we plant now may come to fruition in years to come. We do not always see the results of our labors.

A young woman who loved flowers set out a rare vine beside her back fence. It grew vigorously but did not bloom. Day after day she cultivated it. One morning an invalid neighbor, whose back lot adjoined the young woman's, called, saying, "You can't imagine how much I have been enjoying the blossoms of the vine you planted."

Upon walking around to the neighbor's backyard, the young woman was amazed to see a mass of luxurious flowers on the other side of her fence.

Lord, help us to know our efforts are not in vain. There may be those whose lives we have touched without realizing it, if we could only see on the other side of the fence. Amen.

9
Prayer—The Groundwork

"After they prayed, the place where they were meeting was shaken" (Acts 4:31).

Why don't we see more results from our teaching? A reason for our lack of effectiveness may be traced to the amount of time we spend in prayer, as suggested in the following poem by a missionary who spent her life in China.

Will I Pray?

Sometimes I have so much to do;
   I think it must be done.
I'll work so very, very hard
   From morn till set of sun,
But here is something I have found:
   This really doesn't pay.
I've always found I've weaker grown
   If I have failed to pray.

Sometimes 'twas something for myself,
   Sometimes it was for God,
Sometimes it was for other folks
   That many steps I've trod.
But 'tis no matter who 'twas for,
   I truthfully must say
My faith and trust had smaller grown
   Because I failed to pray.

So I am trying hard to learn

> That nothing's really great
> If it must take my praying time,
>   So praying has to wait.
> It's praying makes me fit to work;
>   It is my staff and stay.
> And work will never be my best
>   If I have failed to pray.
>
> —Silvia Ward

An evangelist once said, "If you get hold of God, then you can get a hold on the people." Certainly this should be true for a Sunday school teacher. We need to pray earnestly and specifically for our students, being alert for the answers and quick to give thanks for them.

Lord, help us to make prayer the foundation of our preparation for our class. Let us reach You in prayer, so we can reach our pupils for You. Amen.

10

Faith To Move Classes

"Now faith is being sure of what we hope for and certain of what we do not see" (Hebrews 11:1).

How much faith do we have that God will answer when we pray? A missionary once preached of God's faithfulness to answer prayer. A little girl, who wanted very badly to go to the mission school, was listening. At the close of the message she asked the missionary to take her back to school with him, but he had to refuse because of lack of funds. "But you pray the Lord will send in more money and I'll pray too," he told her.

When the missionary returned home, he found an unexpected, generous check and, remembering his promise to the girl, sent for her. Though it was normally over a day's journey to the girl's home, the messengers had her back by noon the same day. They said they had met the girl just a few miles from the mission station. She explained. "You said God would answer, and as we both had prayed, I thought I might as well start out."[7]

What challenges does your class present? An "energetic" child? An indifferent teenager? A doubting adult? Take them to Jesus. Prayer changes more than things—it changes people!

And if you need a "primer" to build your faith before you pray, rehearse the answers God gave to people in Scripture. Then rehearse the answers He's given to you. And expect Him to answer again.

Lord, remind us of the many answers You've given to our prayers of the past and may this remembrance build gratitude in our hearts. Make us childlike in our trust as we pray—for we are Your children. Amen.

11

Are We Responsible?

"Whoever turns a sinner from the error of his way will save him from death and cover over a multitude of sins" (James 5:20).

An English criminal was being led to his execution on the scaffold and the prison chaplain shared with him the story of salvation. The prisoner turned to the chaplain and said, "Do you believe that? If you really believe what you say, you ought to go on hands and knees, if necessary, and tell every man in England, personally, your story."[8] The call to personal evangelism means tired feet, aching head, and often a weary heart.

A man on his way to prayer meeting one evening saw a stranger looking into an open window of the church. The Christian introduced himself and invited the man to attend the service. The stranger agreed, and it was the beginning of a new life for him, for that night he was converted.

After the meeting he said to the man who had invited him, "Do you know, I've lived in this city for seven years and no one has ever asked me to go to church. Why, I hadn't been here three days before deliverymen from the bakery, the dairy, and a laundry contacted me. Yet in all those years you are the first person who ever showed an interest in my soul."[9]

A teacher was concerned because a student left after Sunday school without staying for church. Another church member noticed her gazing after the departing student and said, "Don't worry; you aren't responsible for her."

Lord, convince us we are responsible for the spiritual welfare of our pupils. If we don't care, who will? Amen.

12
Looking Beyond the Obvious

"Man looks at the outward appearance, but the Lord looks at the heart" (1 Samuel 16:7).

A story is told of a sculptor who spent his days chipping away at a huge block of marble. He was watched daily by a small boy who sat quietly, his eyes reflecting growing curiosity and wonder. Finally, as the figure of a sleeping lion emerged from the artist's deft strokes, the boy's amazement exploded in the question, "But how did you know that lion was in there?"

We do not know the potential of those individuals sitting in front of us on Sunday mornings. The girl with a torn dress and straggly hair may some day be packing dresses for the missionary society, or unpacking the boxes herself on the mission field. The freckle-faced boy who is always in trouble may become a preacher or a dependable Christian layman.

Look beyond what you can see to what God can see! He looked at Zacchaeus in the sycamore tree and saw a repentant sinner. He looked at Matthew the tax collector and saw a trusted disciple and Gospel writer. He looked at impetuous Peter and saw a Spirit-filled preacher winning thousands of souls to the Lord. He looked at Saul of Tarsus, persecutor of the Christians, and saw Paul, a founder of churches and writer of epistles.

He looked at Billy Sunday the baseball player and saw a dynamic evangelist. He looked at you and saw, among other things, a Sunday school teacher.

Lord, help us to look beyond our students' appearance and behavior and see them as valuable individuals with great potential. Amen.

13
Marked by Love

"Give therefore thy servant an understanding heart" (1 Kings 3:9, KJV).

Teachers can learn a lesson from the common tree trunk. When we look at the trunk of a freshly cut tree we see a series of circles, the rings of the tree. Each of those rings represents a year's growth. If we count them, we will know the age of the tree; but more than this, if we measure the rings, we can determine the rainfall. Weather cycles of long ago are revealed in the rings of very old trees. Thin rings indicate dry seasons; thick rings point to years of heavy rainfall.

There are no rings in the human trunk, but physicians claim that in a postmortem examination they can find evidences of every disease a person has had. Every vitamin deficiency, every accident, every illness, leaves its mark upon the body. A skilled pathologist can find the signs of diseases of years ago: measles, mumps, pneumonia, or liver trouble. The body, like a tree trunk, carries within it the record of its years.

And we wonder—is it the same with our hearts? When the Great Physician looks into them, what does He find? Marks of compassion and concern or marks of complacency and indifference? As we grow spiritually as teachers, do the marks grow thicker, pointing to the fact that we have watered our souls plentifully at the Fountain of Life?

Someone once said, "God will not look you over for medals—but for scars." What scars will we show when we come to the judgment? Will they be scars of remorse or of victory? Will we be able to say, "We have loved"? What marks will be found around our hearts?

Lord, give us understanding hearts, give us loving hearts—hearts that are moved with the needs of our students. Amen.

14
Win Them One by One

"In that day . . . you, O Israelites, will be gathered up one by one" (Isaiah 27:12).

It is so easy to pray, "Lord, save my class." But why not pray for each student individually?

Maybe we don't know if Jill and Randy are Christians, even though their parents may be. Perhaps we have never visited in Rhonda's home because she lives in a rough section of town. Karen seldom attends Sunday school and we've heard she's a little wild. Oh, how much easier to pray, "Lord, save my *class*"!

A teacher was concerned over a seventeen-year-old class member. The girl came from a home where little love was shown, and she could not seem to accept the fact that God loved her. Since she seldom came to Sunday school, it was hard for the teacher to reach her. Then she thought of using the pupil as a babysitter. As the girl spent more time in the teacher's home and saw the love shown in the family, and as she and the teacher became better acquainted, her heart was melted. Eventually the teenager was able to accept God's love for her. All because someone cared.

It may take a little extra on our part to win our pupils. We may have to invite them over for a meal, pick them up for class, or even pay their taxi fare. But if we think of them as individuals and are sensitive to their needs, we can win them one by one.

Lord, help us to find a way to get acquainted with each of our students individually so we may win them to You. Amen.

15
Involved in the Body

"Christ is like a single body, which has many parts" (1 Corinthians 12:12, TEV).

No man is an Iland, intire of it selfe; every man is a peece of the Continent, a part of the maine; if a Clod bee washed away by the Sea, Europe is the lesse, as well as if a Promontorie were, as well as if a Mannor of thy friends or of thine owne were; any mans death diminishes me, because I am involved in Mankinde; And therefore never send to know for whom the bell tolls; It tolls for thee.[10]

It is easy to say, "I am only one, What can I do?" Once during World War II, a pageant was held in the Los Angeles Coliseum to honor the city's war heroes. After a mock battle scene had driven home the seeming helplessness of the individual, silence fell, and the emcee said, "Perhaps you sometimes say to yourself, my job isn't important; it's so little. But you are wrong. The most obscure person can be very important. Let me show you what I mean."

The Coliseum lights were shut off, leaving the arena in total darkness. Then the speaker struck a match and in the blackness the tiny flame could be seen by everyone. "Now you can see the importance of one little light," he said. "Suppose we all strike a light." In an instant, matches were struck all over the stadium until nearly 100,000 pinpoints of light illuminated the summer night. Quickly the audience understood the power of the individual life.

A minister once said, "I never hear a symphony orchestra without thinking of the importance of the individual and the necessity for cooperation. No man can make a symphony orchestra. The combined talents of many musicians, working in harmony and unity, are needed to achieve the desired results."

Lord, may we ever be mindful of the importance of the individual, and of our job as a Sunday school teacher, no matter how insignificant it may seem at times. Amen.

16
Our Investment

" 'Assemble the people before me to hear my words so that they . . . may teach them to their children' " (Deuteronomy 4:10).

Young Chris was spending part of his summer vacation with his grandparents on their farm—one that was still operated on an old-fashioned basis. One morning he watched and wondered as his grandfather worked hard at milking the cows by hand, and then turned around to feed the milk to the calves. It took some time to see reason in the process, but finally he came to a conclusion which seemed valid to him, "I see it now; to get anything out of them when they're old, you have to put a lot into them when they're young."[11]

How much have we put into our students—how much time, how much effort, how much involvement? We should consider the following pledge:

1. I am willing to inconvenience myself for a student.
2. I will begin preparing next week's lesson before Saturday night.
3. I am willing to say, "I don't know."
4. I am equally willing to say, "I'll try to find out."
5. I am willing to follow through on whatever I say I will do—or they'll know the reason why.
6. I am ready to pray for any student, anytime, anyplace.
7. I will look for ways to involve my students in the life of the church.

8. I will try to accept any rejection from my students, forgiving them even though they may not ask.

A young girl had a Sunday school teacher whom she idolized. One day she told her teacher, "I wish I could be the kind of Christian you are." The teacher wisely replied, "Anyone can have just as much of God as he wants."

Lord, help us to draw our students' attention to Jesus Christ, to inspire them to draw closer to Him, and to challenge them to a deeper spiritual life—by the investment we are willing to make in their lives. Amen.

17

Are We Qualified?

"God gave knowledge and understanding of all kinds of literature and learning" (Daniel 1:17).

Qualified teachers are necessary to a successful Sunday school. But how do we determine if *we* are qualified to teach?

Betty Barnett Griffith in her book *The Challenge of Caravan* gives a list of leadership characteristics found in Jesus. She advises, "As you work with your group from week to week, refer to these characteristics often and check to see if you are guiding their lives as Jesus led His followers when He was here on earth."[12]

1. He was a prepared Leader.

2. He did the things that made His group believe in Him.
3. His leadership was characterized by companionship.
4. He treated the members of His group as individuals.
5. He gave them work to do.
6. He made them feel free to come to Him with their difficulties.
7. He asked them questions.
8. He taught them clearly the profound truths of life.
9. He took time to be with them.
10. He was open to their suggestions.
11. He and His group had an intimate bond of attachment each for the other.
12. He drew His lesson material in part from incidents as they arose.
13. They ate together as friends.
14. He used object lessons in teaching.
15. He depended on His Heavenly Father for wisdom, understanding, and grace.
16. He established himself in their memories.
17. He prayed for them.[13]

Lord, may we look to You, the Great Teacher, for our example. May we depend on You for wisdom, understanding, and strength. Let us be established in our students' memories as teachers who love God and, in turn, are able to love them. Amen.

18
With Many Parables

"With many . . . parables Jesus spoke the word to them, as much as they could understand" (Mark 4:33).

Jesus taught in many different ways. He used object lessons ("Show me the coin"—Matthew 22:19), stories ("There was a man who had two sons"—Matthew 21:28), dramatization ("It's a ghost"—Matthew 14:26), questions ("Who do you say I am?"—Matthew 16:15). His objective was to impart understanding. But He knew He had to get the people's attention and teach on their level.

Have you ever thought about your approach? There are two basic orientations in teaching: an orientation toward the learner (also called student-centered) and an orientation toward the teacher (also called teacher-centered).

The development of a teacher-centered class is not unusual. The teacher is a natural focal point. It can go to an extreme, though—from the presentation of the lesson to the arrangement of chairs.

For actual learning, however, the more effective orientation is toward the student. This approach is more likely to involve the student in whatever class activity occurs. As a matter of fact, another term for the student-oriented approach is "involvement learning."

Such an approach will counter the complaint one little boy had of his class: "We never do anything there."

Everyone, not just little children, likes to be involved,

to be taken into consideration, to be included in shaping the class.

Whenever you can, get the participation of your students. The more you involve their senses, their minds, the greater will be their learning. Remember, the teacher hasn't taught until the learner has learned.

Lord, what a teacher was Your Son! Help me to catch the attention of my students the way He did. And then give me the understanding they need so I can pass it along.

19
Leading the Leader

"John was standing with two of his disciples when Jesus passed by. John . . . said, 'There is the Lamb of God.' The two disciples heard him say this, and followed Jesus" (John 1:35-37, NEB).

In Bible times the man was the acknowledged leader of his family. Joshua reflected this when he said, "As for me and my household, we will serve the Lord" (Joshua 24:15).

In any group, formal or not, there is at least an *unspoken* leader. Whatever he or she does, most of the others will follow in some way.

A teacher of junior highs said to an evangelist, "Unless I can see my pupils saved in this meeting, I shall surely die!" She had worked hard to bring new members into her class, but none had been converted. She fasted and prayed for wisdom. If only she could influence the key girl to make the first move. She talked about the church revival to her class and they set a night to attend as a body. To make it easier she invited the whole class to her home for supper, then they would go to the church together.

On the appointed night the evangelist prayed for special guidance as he saw the junior highs and their teacher file in—two entire rows of them—lively, attractive teenagers. At the close of the sermon an invitation was given. There was a pause. Quietly the teacher slipped her arm around the girl who was the leader. In a moment that girl started forward. Another came, then others, until every pupil was kneeling for prayer. It was a beautiful sight—a whole class and their teacher praying together.

The teacher was overjoyed. To the evangelist she said, "You know this has been the hardest day's work I ever did, but it's the biggest day's pay I ever had."[14]

Lord, help us to recognize the leaders in our classes so with Your help we can channel their influence for You. Amen.

20

Never Alone

"Do not fear, for I am with you; do not be dismayed, for I am your God. I will strengthen you and help you" (Isaiah 41:10).

What do we do when we are tempted to be discouraged and we want to quit? There are many times in our work when we feel so alone.

A farmer was plowing in his field with just one horse, a huge animal that wore large blinders that prevented him from seeing either to the right or to the left. Some people from the city had stopped to get a picture of the quaint scene when they heard the farmer calling out to the horse, as though he had a variety of names: "Get up there, Joe. Come on, Dan. Get a move on you, Bill. Jerry, Spot, move along there."

Unable to restrain their curiosity, the sightseers asked for an explanation. "It's that big old horse," the farmer said. "He is so strong that he doesn't know his own strength. So I put blinders on him to keep him from looking around; then I call out several other names and he thinks he is working with all of them. If he knew he was pulling the whole load, he would give up in a minute. But when he thinks he has others helping, he goes right along and does the whole job himself."

An evangelist once suggested that when we are discouraged, and think we are alone, we should consider

Shadrach, Meshach, and Abednego in the fiery furnace,
Caleb and Joshua who said, "We are able to go over,"
Daniel in the lions' den,
Paul and Silas in jail at midnight,
Luther, Wesley, and others who made it through,
and take courage.[15]

Lord, You promised You would never leave us or forsake us. You have called us to teach. As You have been with others You will be with us. Thank You. Amen.

21
More Than We Can Imagine

"To him who is able to do immeasurably more than all we ask or imagine . . ." (Ephesians 3:20).

When we pray, do we ask largely enough? A pastor was very concerned about a large debt on his church and he made it a matter of earnest prayer. A stranger called on him one day and said he had heard about the problem and wanted to help. He laid a blank check on the pastor's desk, saying, "Fill in the amount you need and I'll be back later to sign it."

The pastor thought, *He doesn't know how much we need. I'll just put down half the amount.* Within an hour the man returned, gave the check a hasty glance, signed it, and hurried away. The pastor, looking at the check, recognized the name of a very well-known and wealthy philanthropist who could easily have given the entire amount the church needed. "Oh, man of little faith," he exclaimed, "Oh, man of little faith."[16]

Andrew Murray, in his book *With Christ in the School of Prayer,* says:

> We have become so accustomed to limiting the wonderful love and the large promises of our God. . . . If there is one thing I think the church needs to learn, it is that God means for prayer to have an answer.[17]

How "imaginative" have you been in your prayers for your class? Has some aspect of teaching got you stymied? Imagine what God can do. Just imagine!

Lord, we ask You for so little, when you want to give us so much. Help us to remember we pray in the human tense; You answer in the divine. Amen.

22
Only a Boy

"Another of his disciples, Andrew, . . . spoke up, 'Here is a boy with five small barley loaves and two small fish' " (John 6:8,9).

A cartoon appeared in a Boston newspaper some years ago on the anniversary of Lincoln's birth. The cartoon was titled "Hardin County, 1809," and pictured two men in conversation.

"What's new in your county, Neighbor?" inquired the one.

"Nothing, nothing at all—except for a new baby down in Tom Lincoln's log cabin. Nothing important ever happens in these deserted hills of ours."

A drummer boy slipped and fell from a cliff when Napoleon's army was crossing the Alps. An officer came to Napoleon and asked if they should pause and learn the boy's fate and rescue him if he was alive. The leader's reply was, "No, it's only a boy. March on." Evidently Napoleon had forgotten that he too was once "only a boy."[18]

Does this sound familiar? A revival is scheduled and completed. Someone asks another about the meeting and the reply is, "Only one boy went forward." Only one boy!

We have become so accustomed to thinking in large numbers. Sure, it was great in the Early Church when three thousand were added in one day. But remember, that was due to the obedience of one person—Peter— one person who was once "only a boy."

Lord, help us realize the importance You place on that one boy or one girl in our class. Whether they become great or ordinary in men's eyes, help us prize them as Your creation, in Your image. Amen.

23
Loving the Unlovely

"May the Lord make your love increase and overflow for each other and for everyone else, just as ours does for you" (1 Thessalonians 3:12).

A young woman who disliked bugs, or anything that crawled, began dating a college student who was majoring in science. Part of his work involved collecting various insects and studying their habits. As the relationship between the two young people deepened, and the naturalist began to teach the woman more about the insects he was studying, she also became interested in them.

One day she exclaimed, "They were once so ugly to me, but since I learned to love Jim, he has taught me how beautiful they can be."

Leonard Bolton, pioneer missionary to southwest China, received a different perspective on the problem of unattractiveness. Beginning to struggle with revulsion at the filthiness of the Tibetan people, Bolton cried out in prayer.

> That night the Lord spoke to me in a dream. I saw a filthy individual standing before me, draped in an assortment of rags. Everything about him was repulsive. I exclaimed, "This must be one of the filthiest persons I've ever seen!"
>
> Then the Lord Jesus spoke softly, "Leonard, that is how *you* appeared in My sight. . . . Before my precious blood was applied. . . ."[19]

Lord, help us to love our students as You have loved us, that through our love they may find new life in You. Amen.

24
Go Out

"The master told his servant, 'Go out to the roads and country lanes' " (Luke 14:23).

Much of a Sunday school teacher's evangelism may be done outside the classroom—first, because many who need it the most probably won't come to church, and, second, because there isn't always time in the class period to give attention to all the questions and needs of the students. The teacher should be willing to pursue a student beyond classroom walls.

Dwight L. Moody's life for Christ was the fruit of a Sunday school ministry. One morning eighteen-year-old Moody, a farm boy turned shoe salesman, walked into a Sunday school class in a Boston church. The teacher, Edward Kimball, made him feel at home, easing the first awkward moments when young Dwight could not find the book of John in a borrowed Bible.

In succeeding months, Moody attended faithfully and Kimball's teaching took root in his heart. One Saturday morning the teacher felt he should speak to the boy personally about his need of Christ. Going to the shoe store, he found Moody in the stockroom wrapping shoes. Quietly and with tear-filled eyes, he asked the boy to come to Christ. Moody did, and the rest is history.[20]

Lord, help us to realize You are not restricted to a classroom. Compel us to go out so others may be compelled to come in. Amen.

25
Sharing Your Life

"You observed the sort of life we lived . . . and . . . were led to become imitators of us" (1 Thessalonians 1:5,6, *Jerusalem Bible*).

Personal contact does not necessarily mean a visit to the student's home. We can invite the students to *our* home—as a class and also as individuals. One teacher of primary girls had a "bake-in" where the girls were allowed to bake a small cake and take it home. Slumber parties and camping trips are popular with children and teens.

We can invite our students to our home on their birthdays and serve their favorite foods, or discover their hobbies and invite them to a ballgame or an art exhibit. A small gift or activity planned especially for the individual will be appreciated more than an identical gift for each student.

If you have a full-time job, lack of time may be a problem. If you teach teenagers or adults you could hire a student to do babysitting, spring cleaning, yard work, home or auto repairs—or to teach you something, like playing a musical instrument or crocheting.

"Like father, like son" is no empty saying. The apostle Paul knew the force of example. He deliberately shared his life with believers. He often had young men accompany him for training on his tours of ministry. They picked up as much from his life as they did from his teaching. He told the believers at Corinth, Philippi, and Thessalonica, "Imitate me" (1 Corinthians 4:16; Philippians 3:17; 2 Thessalonians 3:7). Because Paul had *lived* among them, they knew what he meant.

Lord, help us to share our lives with our students so we may clarify the gospel for them.

26
Study To Be Approved

"Present yourself to God as one approved, a workman who does not need to be ashamed and who correctly handles the word" (2 Timothy 2:15).

Preparation is more than just reading the lesson in the quarterly. We need to continually add to our knowledge by getting acquainted with the great writers and reading newspapers, magazines, and commentaries. Illustrations from these sources are more suitable than an overdose of personal examples.

We should be familiar with the names of people and cities in the lesson and know how to pronounce them. We should have a Bible map in the classroom to point out the location of the lesson sites. God's Word tells us, "My people are destroyed for lack of knowledge" (Hosea 4:6). We cannot afford to lose a student because of shallow lesson preparation and errors in our presentation.

During World War II, a mountain boy joined the army. He had never seen an M-1 rifle before and it was somewhat confusing to him. But as soon as he learned the knack of operating the weapon, he set a new army record for sharpshooting. The astonished officers asked him how he did it.

"Well, sir, it's like this. There are fifteen in our family and we've always had a hard time scraping together enough to eat. Every morning Pop would hand me the old gun and *one* bullet. 'Here, son,' he would say, 'go out and get us some breakfast.' So you see, sir, I haven't been used to doing much missing."[21]

Lord, our visitor may not return and our regulars may be discouraged and ready to drop out. Help us to get our guns loaded and be prepared, for we may get only one shot, and we can't afford to do much missing. Amen.

27
A Cry of Prayer

"The Spirit himself intercedes for us with groans that words cannot express" (Romans 8:26).

Three brothers—twelve, ten, and four—and their five-year-old sister were walking along the shore of a lake one day when the little girl slipped and fell into deep water. The oldest brother, with the help of the next oldest, was able to bring her out to safety. Later when their father questioned them about the near tragedy, the ten-year-old said, "I laid down on the bank and when Martin got close enough, I took hold of his coat and helped pull him out."

"That was good cooperation," commended the father. Then he asked the four-year-old what he did to help. "Oh, Daddy," the little boy replied, "I just cried and cried."[22]

As we kneel in prayer, holding our classbooks before us, and the faces begin to appear in our minds—with their problems and spiritual needs—we may not always know how to pray. But we have the Spirit. When we falter in knowing what to pray for our students, let us expect the Spirit to express their needs to God—even if it is only to "cry and cry."

Lord, thank You for the Holy Spirit's ministry in our lives as teachers. May we learn to depend on Him to make us equal to our task. Amen.

28
The Day of Small Things

"Who despises the day of small things?" (Zechariah 4:10).

A girl came home from school one day crying because she had been given only a small part in the children's program while her best friend got the leading role. After drying her tears, her grandfather took out his pocket watch and put it in the little girl's hand. "What do you see?" he asked.

"A silver case, a face, and two hands," the girl replied.

Turning the watch over and opening the back, the grandfather repeated the question. The girl said she saw many tiny wheels. "This watch would be useless," the grandfather said, "without every part—even the ones you can hardly see." That object lesson helped the girl all through life to see the importance of the small duties we are asked to perform.[23]

An elderly lady, born in Germany, did not have the education to be a Sunday school teacher; however, she was faithful in attendance even though she had to walk two miles to get there. She was not a good reader nor a writer nor a singer. But she loved to take fresh eggs and strawberries to the parsonage, which she did often. At her funeral, the pastor used as his text, "She hath done what she could."

> Is your place a small place?
> Tend it with care—
> He set you there.

> Is your place a large place?
> Guard it with care—
> He set you there.
> What e'er your place, it is
> Not yours alone, but His
> Who set you there.
> —John Oxenham[24]

Lord, we may not be able to draw or write or sing. But we can study our lesson; we can love our students and do little things for them; we can pray for each one by name during the week. And what we can do, help us to do, as unto You. Amen.

29
"He Puts the Waddle in the Duck"

"A cheerful heart is good medicine" (Proverbs 17:22).

The Bible contains no lengthy passages on humor, lightheartedness, or being generally upbeat about life—only a verse here and there. Perhaps the people of the Bible simply understood that a smile was more pleasant than a frown, a laugh more healthy than a harrumph.

Perhaps too it was enough for them to hear the refrain "It was good" throughout the creation story, and that "the morning stars sang together and all the angels shouted for joy" (Job 38:7). God did a great job and had everything under control.

Elaine Curzio, contemporary singer/composer, also drew her conclusions about humor and God from observing His creation, putting her question in the title of her song: "Does God Ever Laugh?"

> He puts the waddle in the duck.
> A giraffe's neck gets stuck.
> Owl's eyes they bulge at you and me.
> A camel's back is humped
> Kangaroos, they jump.
> If they make me laugh,
> Then why not He*

Unfortunately Christianity has had its share of sourpusses, or at least those who made the mistake of thinking *serious* meant *grim*. There is no question that the Bible deals with the most important issue a person will ever consider: his relationship to God. But the Bible, after all, calls its message *good* news. And for those who receive it, it should mean joy, happiness, lightheartedness—Yea, God!

Children are especially susceptible to their teacher's overall demeanor. Teenagers sometimes wonder about it. And adults are at least subconsciously affected. If you are pleasant, congenial, and allow yourself a sense of humor, you will find your students disposed to believe that God's message really *is* good news.

---

*© MCMLXX by Vanguard Music Corp., 1595 Broadway, New York, N.Y. 10019. Reprinted by permission Vanguard Music Corp. Further reproduction prohibited. A piano-vocal arrangement is available from the publisher and a recording by Avant Garde Records can be obtained from the same address.

Lord, help us to show the joy that is inherent in Your salvation.

30
Doers—Not Just Hearers

"Do not merely listen to the word. . . . Do what it says" (James 1:22).

A young book salesman was assigned to a rural area. Seeing a farmer seated in a rocking chair on his front porch, the young man approached him with all the zeal of a newly trained salesman. "Sir," he said, "I have a book that will tell you how to farm ten times better than you are doing it now."

The farmer stopped rocking, looked at the young fellow, and said, "Son, I don't need your book. I already know how to farm ten times better than I'm doing it now."[25]

A woman walked into a writers seminar and looked at the variety of books on display. Leafing through one of the books, she commented, "I could read all these books and it still wouldn't make me a writer." How right she was. And it's the same with teaching.

We can go through any Christian bookstore and buy a large selection of books and tapes on Sunday school teaching. We can watch films and attend workshops on working with children. But taking advantage of these doesn't automatically make us teachers. Many of us already know how to teach "ten times better" than we are doing it now.

The secret is in knowing *and* doing! The ideas we read are effective *only* when we put them into practice. As someone said, "We don't need more light; we need only to walk in the light we now have." Teachers, we don't need more books or speakers or workshops, although these are encouraging. We need to take our notes from our steno pads and demonstrate them before our students. Then we will see results.

Lord, thank You for all the books and films and workshops. Now, give us a push—from wanting to be an effective teacher to actually being one. Amen.

31
Let the Children Come

"Let the little children come to me" (Matthew 19:14).

There was a good spirit in a junior fellowship meeting one Sunday evening. Several had raised their hands for prayer. In the benediction the leader prayed, "Lord, if there is anyone here without Thee, help me to pray for him this week until he has Jesus in his heart."

The meeting was over, and the juniors were urged to stay for the following worship service, which many of them did. After the service, as the junior leader began to leave the church, she felt someone tugging at her coat. Turning, she saw one of her junior girls with tears in her eyes. "Teacher, will you pray for me this week?"

The leader's arm went around the girl and she replied, "I'll pray for you right now if you want me too." The two took off their coats and, hand in hand, walked back up to the front of the church. There the junior girl accepted Jesus.

A few weeks passed. The girl told others of her newfound faith and seemed very happy. Then one night she came into the auditorium, her face shining. "I got a surprise," she said to the leader. "Wait until church." The leader waited, and just before the evening service began she saw the reason for the girl's happiness. Her father was in church! When the invitation was given, he was one of the first to go forward, followed by his wife.

"Will you pray for me this week?" A simple request. It took only a few moments, but a family was won for Christ.

Lord, thank You for alerting us to the importance of children. Help us never to ignore them. Amen.

32
The Teacher as Evangelist

"He gave some to be apostles, some to be prophets, some to be evangelists, and some to be pastors and teachers, to prepare God's people for works of service" (Ephesians 4:11,12).

A Sunday school teacher may function quite naturally as an evangelist. Remember how Dwight L. Moody came to Christ through the earnest efforts of his Sunday school teacher (see the devotional "Go Out")? The following paraphrase of 1 Corinthians 13, prepared by an unknown author, encourages this thought:

> Though I speak with the tongues of scholarship, and though I use approved methods of education, and fail to win my pupils to Christ, I become as a cloud of mist in an open sea, as the moan of the wind in a Syrian desert.
>
> And though I read all Sunday school literature, and attend Sunday school conventions and institutes, and summer schools, and yet am satisfied with less than winning to Christ and establishing my pupils in Christian character and service, it profiteth me nothing.
>
> The soul-winning teacher, the character-building teacher, suffereth long and is kind; he envieth not others who are free from the teaching task; he vaunteth not himself, is not puffed up with intellectual pride.
>
> Such a teacher doth not behave unseemingly between Sundays, seeketh not his own comfort, is not easily provoked.
>
> Beareth all things, believeth all things, hopeth all things.
>
> And now abideth knowledge, methods, evangelism, these three; but the greatest of these is evangelism.

The oil producer does not say, "Give me petroleum that is already refined." The steelmaker does not demand premelted ore. Each expects to take crude or unfinished resources and refine them.

Developing the potential of a person is all part of evangelism: finding him, leading him to Christ, teaching him to mature in his Christian life, preparing him for "works of service."

Lord, help us not to limit ourselves unnecessarily in our role of teacher. When it involves evangelism, help us to take the initiative. Amen.

33
Laborers With God

"Each will be rewarded according to his own labor. For we are God's fellow workers" (1 Corinthians 3:8,9).

The camp kitchen had no modern conveniences. The water had to be hauled in and heated on a woodburning cookstove and the steam from the copper boiler made the summer heat unbearable.

Marian, a young Christian teenager, plunged her hands into the huge dishpan of stinging soapsuds and looked with despair at the endless stacks of dirty dishes and piles of black pots and pans. All had to be scoured, washed, and dried by hand. Her preacher dad was manager of the camp, and that meant his whole family had become involved in the work. Marian and her sister had been assigned to do dishes.

As she worked, she could hear the people at the meeting some distance away, singing and rejoicing. She longed to be with them, enjoying the blessings and glory of the Lord. But instead, the sweat from her forehead and her salty tears mixed with the dishwater. She felt too frustrated even to pray.

Suddenly she was aware of God's presence. It was as if Someone were standing right beside her saying, "Marian, don't cry. I understand. When the final rewards are given, your reward will be as big and as important as the camp evangelist's."[26]

This story reminds us of another preacher and his wife who for a number of years worked with the children at the church camp. In the amphitheater where the children met, the workers could hear the singing from the main tabernacle. Surely they missed being with their friends and fellow ministers, but God had called—and their work with the children bore fruit.

Lord, in teaching, especially in teaching children, we forfeit being with our peers in a class. Help us to accept this, to be fellow workers with You. Amen.

34

The Personal Touch

" 'Zacchaeus, . . . I must stay at your house today' " (Luke 19:5).

"How can we show an individual we care?" we may ask. The best way is by personal contact. Everyone likes to be visited. We may say, "But I don't have time for personal calls. Children love to get mail. I'll just send the absentee a card and tell him I miss him."

Children (and adults) do enjoy getting cards, it's true. But how much better if we put on the card, "I'll be over to see you Saturday afternoon." He may keep the card for a week or two but the memory of our visit, the fact that we cared enough to visit, will stay with him for a lifetime.

Personal contact can also provide many answers for a teacher. Is a pupil a problem in class? Does he seek attention by goofing off, giving smart answers, or monopolizing the discussion?

A visit to the home will reveal the number of children in the family, financial conditions, the absence of a parent, and the spiritual atmosphere of the home. All these factors influence the pupil's behavior.

Or it may be an adult member is too shy to answer a question or read the Scripture passage, or is irregular in attendance. A visit may find an invalid parent or a retarded child, or financial difficulties that do not allow the student to dress as he would like for Sunday school.

Be it our star pupil or our biggest headache, a personal visit to him will open our eyes and give us insight as we prepare our lessons. Perhaps next week's discussion can be *subtly* guided so that that pupil will receive help with his problems. And a visit will help us to be specific in our prayers as we pray for family needs as well as individual problems.

Lord, help us to take time to make that visit, knowing that personal contact brings the best results. Amen.

35
Diamonds in the Rough

"They shall be mine, saith the Lord of hosts, in that day when I make up my jewels" (Malachi 3:17, KJV).

"When in Amsterdam, Holland, one summer," says a traveler, "I was interested in a visit we made to a place famous for polishing diamonds. We saw the men engaged in the work. When a diamond is found it is rough and dark like a common pebble. It takes a long time to polish it, and it is very hard work.

"It is held by means of a piece of metal close to the surface of a large wheel, which is kept going round and round. Fine diamond dust is put on this wheel, nothing else being hard enough to polish the diamond. This work is kept up for months, and sometimes for several years, before it is finished. If the diamond is intended for a king, then greater time and trouble are spent upon it."[27]

Billy was not raised in a Christian home. He never knew his father. But when Billy was sixteen, an older lady in the town became concerned for Billy and his three friends. Unable to drive, she paid for their taxi fare so they could be in church. During a revival Billy was converted. After high school he attended Bible college, then seminary, and later became a minister. A "diamond in the rough."

It doesn't happen all at once. We may feel like we're going "round and round" sometimes, but we must hold the student close to our heart. The work may have to be kept up for months, and sometimes for several years before it is finished.

Lord, help us to spend greater time and trouble, for these jewels are intended for the King. Amen.

36
Time To Teach

"There is a time for everything, and a season for every activity under heaven" (Ecclesiastes 3:1).

One hour a week! But how much of that hour is actually spent in teaching? Let's look at a typical class period: The students come into the classroom and immediately there is a loud roar of conversation. When everyone finally settles down, there may be a brief opening—one or two songs, prayer, etc.

Next comes the taking of the attendance, either orally or with the teacher doing it silently, while the pupils start visiting again. Then the basket is passed for the offering, and that is counted.

The next item is announcements, usually of a social nature. What kind of party? Where? When? Finally a date is set, and we can begin the lesson. But part-way through, someone comes to the door for the attendance and offering. Sound familiar? It doesn't have to be.

We can start our opening on time, *no matter* how many are there. During this time an assistant can be quietly taking the attendance and counting the offering which the pupils dropped into a container as they entered the room. The assistant can then take the attendance book and offering to the Sunday school office. The class president can make any announcements which have been decided by a social committee during the week; we can then start the lesson and proceed with no interruptions. God can work much better in such an atmosphere than in the confusion of the first example.

Lord, may our teaching time not be displaced by secondary activities. Rather, help us to be creative in doing those things that are necessary so we can give first place to actual teaching. Amen.

37

The Comforter Is Come

"I will ask the Father, and he will give you another Counselor. . . . I will not leave you" (John 14:16,18).

A new sanctuary was being built and the pastor wanted to have it ready for Easter Sunday. It was Saturday—only one more day to complete the job.

The minister assigned to his son the task of gathering up the loose bricks around the front yard and taking them to the back. He gave him a big wheelbarrow for the task. Pushing it empty was a big enough task for the lad, let alone filled with bricks. Time and again the wheelbarrow overturned. The boy was getting more and more discouraged, when out of nowhere came a big, burly army sergeant.

"What's the trouble, son?" he asked. The boy explained the situation—that all the bricks had to be removed before the next day. The muscular sergeant threw a load of bricks into the wheelbarrow, marched around to the back of the church, and in no time at all returned for another load. In just a short time the entire job was done.

The boy went to tell his father that the work was completed and the father praised him for getting the job done in record time. Not wanting to take all the credit, the boy said, "But, Father, you don't understand. I didn't do it all myself. This big army sergeant came and helped me."

"Son," the father replied, putting his arm around the boy's shoulders, "Who do you think sent that sergeant?"

We have a big job to do. But we have a big God, and He has sent His Holy Spirit to help us.

Lord, help us to look to You when the load is too heavy, when the pupils don't respond, when we feel like giving up. Help us to pray more! love more! evangelize more! And thank You for sending a Helper. Amen.

38
Where Is the Oboe?

"In the church God has appointed . . . teachers" (1 Corinthians 12:28).

Sir Michael Costa was rehearsing with a large orchestra. Amid the thunder of the organ and the roll of drums, the player of the oboe said to himself, "In all this noise my little instrument doesn't matter," and he ceased playing. Suddenly the great conductor threw up his arms, and all was still. "Where is the oboe?" he cried.[28]

Every one of us is important in God's sight. One minister said, "We are all part of the body of Christ. In our physical body we have small organs such as the spleen and pancreas. They can't be seen, but ask a diabetic and he will tell you the importance of a properly functioning pancreas. We can't all be a heart or a lung in God's kingdom. Some of us have to be content to be a spleen."

Never say you don't do much in the church. Never say "I'm *just* a Sunday school teacher." In the symphony of God's plan, you are necessary. More than any orchestra needs oboes God's kingdom needs teachers.

We can't say, "It doesn't matter if I quit. I won't be missed." If we lay down our quarterly and cease working, the Great Conductor will throw up His arms and cry, "Where is the teacher?"

Lord, help us to have a high view of being a teacher—no matter what age we teach. Help us to view our work as a calling from You. Amen.

39
Welcome Home, Children

"Rejoice that your names are written in heaven" (Luke 10:20).

A Christian railroad engineer was speaking to a group of fellow workers about heaven. "Many years ago as I neared the end of my run each night," he said, "I would always let out a long blast with the whistle just as I'd come around the last curve. Then I'd look up at the familiar little cottage at the top of the hill. My mother and father would be standing in the doorway waving to me. After I had passed, they'd go back inside and say, 'Thank God, Benny is home safe again tonight.'

"Well, they are gone now, and no one is there to welcome me. But someday when I have finished my 'earthly run' and I draw near to heaven's gate, I believe I'll see my precious mother and dad waiting there for me. And one will turn to the other and say, 'Thank God, Benny is home safe at last.' "[29]

Will we be able to say this about our students? After the attendance records have been marked, the offering taken, the announcements made, have we taken the time to explain how to find God?

Sometimes we get so used to having the same students there every Sunday, we assume they know all the answers. But even though they know all the "right words," they may not know how to apply them to their own lives. And the visitor may find confusing the terms that we use every day. Let us take pains to clarify our terms and to regularly explain how to invite God into one's life.

Lord, someday when we near heaven's gate, let us be able to say, "Thank God, all my class is home safe at last." Amen.

40
Who Cares?

"No one is concerned for me. . . . No one cares for my life" (Psalm 142:4).

The author once became acquainted with a lady who obviously had had a very hard life. She had three children, a boy and girl seven and eight, and an infant. Another girl had died of burns received by getting too close to a trash burner.

This had happened only a short time before, and the mother was still very tenderhearted. When invited to go to church, she immediately showed interest and for several months we picked her up every Sunday. The two older children soon both came to the altar in junior church to pray.

One evening the mother also came forward and gave a good testimony afterwards. The family came regularly for a month or so after that and then suddenly quit. Seeing the woman one day in the store I asked why she didn't come anymore, and she replied: "No one really cared about me. They said hello to me when I came to church, but no one ever came to my house. No one ever came to visit. I just didn't feel like anyone cared about me."

This reflected not only upon the author—what about the woman's Sunday school teacher? What about the children's teacher? Why didn't they follow up when the family was absent? The boy had sent away to Billy Graham for a Bible and read it avidly, saying in junior church that he wanted to be a preacher. Where is he now?

Lord, if someone in our class has been absent for a while, help us to find out why. Help us to show our students that we care. Amen.

41
Bands of Love

"I drew them . . . with bands of love" (Hosea 11:4, KJV).

It was a time of "severe mental anguish" for George Matthenson, Scottish minister and hymnwriter. He needed for himself an expression of God's love—and it came forth as a hymn, in "only about five minutes."

> O Love that wilt not let me go,
> I rest my weary soul in Thee;
> I give Thee back the life I owe
> That in Thine ocean depths its flow
> May richer, fuller be.

A teacher in Massachusetts said, "When I introduce myself to new students, I put my name and phone number on the board for them to copy. Then I tell them I am available to them at any time they need me, or if they just want to talk to someone. One time a girl called when her mother went to the hospital and in following this up, her mother received Christ."

What is the key to successful teaching? The answer could be found in the following story: It was a cold Sunday in Chicago in D. L. Moody's Sunday school. Arriving late was a little boy. His bare legs were blue from cold. His coat didn't fit and was held shut with a safety pin. He had no hat or socks, and his shoes were worn.

A greeter began to massage his legs for stimulation and in talking to him discovered he lived over two miles away. "Why did you come this far?" the greeter said. "You must have passed a dozen Sunday schools on the way."

The boy replied, "I guess, sir, it's because they love a feller over here."[30]

Lord, how far would a person come to attend our Sunday school class, based only on the love we show? Help us to bind them to You with bands of love. Amen.

42

A Better Teacher

"So that the body of Christ may be built up . . ." (Ephesians 4:12).

A small boy had been in trouble all day. In the morning he had broken a neighbor's window while playing baseball. At the lunch table he had teased his little sister and made her cry. On and on it went. Finally his mother made him go to bed without his dinner. "Don't forget your prayers," she reminded him, suggesting that he include a plea for God to make him a better boy.

As he knelt by the side of his bed, his mother heard him say, "Dear God, please make me a better boy if you can, but if you can't, never mind, 'cause I'm having an awful good time like I am."[31]

Do we sincerely want God to make us better teachers or are we "having an awful good time" like we are? Hazel A. Lewis, in *Planning for Children in Your Church,* suggests that we "(1) spend at least two hours a week in lesson preparation, beginning early in the week; (2) be present at least ten minutes in advance of the opening of the session; (3) call in the homes . . . during the first two months of the church school year and during the year when possible or necessary; (4) participate in church life and worship; (5) read two books from a suggested list each year, or one book and a monthly magazine; . . . (6) take at least one leadership training course each year; (7) attend monthly workers' conferences."

She concludes, "The desire for growth must come from within. . . . No one is ever completely trained; it is an on-going process as certainly for the teacher as for a doctor or a scientist."[32]

Lord, give us the desire to grow, to improve our methods, to seek more training and, for the edification of Your church, to be a better teacher. Amen.

43
Pedestrian Grace

"Those who hope in the Lord will renew their strength. . . . They will run and not grow weary, and they will walk and not be faint" (Isaiah 40:31).

For some of us it may not be the big problems that get us down, but the routine, the constant plodding, the Sunday-after-Sunday sessions with the same students. Isaiah might have been thinking of this when he wrote, "They will *walk* and not be faint," which a minister once referred to as "pedestrian grace."

"I can plod," said William Carey, the father of modern missions, near the end of his life. "That is my only genius. I can persevere in any definite pursuit. To this I owe everything."

Most of us have heard the name of Ty Cobb, one of baseball's greatest players. He had a 24-year batting average of .367, played in 3,033 games, was at bat 11,429 times, and scored 2,244 runs. He was the batting champion 12 years. Cobb said, "I played hard, applied myself, and tried to do my best in every game."

Shouldn't we as teachers also be able to say, "I worked hard, applied myself to the lesson, and tried to do my best in every class session"? Don't think about running—or even jogging—the distance. Just concentrate on walking. If an occasional sprint is necessary, you'll get the divine energy for it. Otherwise stick to a deliberate, consistent walk.

Lord, help us not to worry about the "running" in our lives, but to concentrate on the everyday walking. At the end of our class session, and at the end of our day, help us to commit it all to You. Amen.

44
A Show of Faith

"Someone will say, 'You have faith; I have deeds.' Show me your faith without deeds, and I will show you my faith by what I do" (James 2:18).

Two boys were going to be late for Sunday school. One boy said, "Let's kneel down and pray."

"No," replied the other, "let's pray as we run."[33]

A man was praying for a friend in need. "Lord, lay your hand on him," he prayed, upon which the Lord replied, "*You* are my hand."

The only way our students will know if we love them is by our actions. We need to pray for them daily, but if we see them in need and do nothing, if we never call, if we do not add feet to our prayers, our prayers are in vain. Sometimes we need to pray and run at the same time.

An itinerant preacher once preached on the subject, "What kind of religion do you have?" He used the three points, (1) Do you have religion? (2) Do you have the catchin' kind? (3) How many have caught it from you?[34]

> I'd rather see a lesson than hear one any day,
> I'd rather one would walk with me than merely tell the way;
> The eye's a better pupil and more willing than the ear,
> Fine counsel is confusing, but example's always clear;
> The best of all the teachers are the ones who live their creeds,
> For to see good put in action is what everybody needs.
>
> I soon can learn to do it, if you'll let me see it done,
> I can watch your hands in action, your tongue too fast may run;
> The lectures you deliver may be very wise and true,
> But I'd rather get my lessons by observing what you do;
> I may not understand the high advice you give,
> But there's no misunderstanding how you act and how you live.

(Adapted from "The Living Sermon," author unknown.)

Lord, we say we believe. Help us to follow through on what we say, and show we believe. Amen.

45
The Hardening of Sin

"Encourage one another . . . so that none of you may be hardened by sin's deceitfulness" (Hebrews 3:13).

A. S. London in his book *Youth Evangelism* tells of sitting in an audience of more than ten thousand people and seeing only one man lift his hand in response to the question as to how many people were converted and came into the church after the age of fifty.

Later in the same book he comments, "It is a very sad condition . . . that only one of every five that come into our Sunday school classes is won to Christ while in the school. One more is finally brought to Christ after he gets away from his class work. But three out of the five are never converted. They are lost to the church world."[35]

This book was written in 1935. The figures may be different today, but it is still a fact that the longer a person resists the lord, the less likely he is to be won.

> I took a piece of plastic clay
> And idly fashioned it one day;
> And as my fingers pressed it, still,
> It moved and yielded to my will.
>
> I came again when days were past,
> The bit of clay was hard at last;
> The form I gave it still it bore
> But I could change that form no more.
>
> I took a piece of living clay
> And gently formed it day by day;

And molded with my power and art,
A young child's soft and yielding heart.

I came again when years were gone,
It was a man I looked upon;
He still that early impress wore,
And I could change him never more.

("My Finished Work," Author unknown)

Lord, help us to reach the children while they are young and pliable, before the day comes when they can no longer be molded. Amen.

46

To the Unknown Teacher

"You are my servant; O Israel, I will not forget you" (Isaiah 44:21).

Upon graduation from college a gifted young man offered himself as a missionary for service in Africa. There were those who felt he was throwing his life away and burying his great talents in the ground. To one of these protesting friends he said:

"In the building of a bridge, before the great span can be thrown across the river, one must first build a foundation. For this, immense boulders are dumped into the water. Most of them are submerged and utterly forgotten. But without them no bridge could be built. I am willing to be such a boulder, submerged and forgotten, if upon me can rest a span that will be part of the bridge of understanding and friendship between my country and Africa."[36]

Robert Morrison, famed missionary to China, and John R. Mott, whose foreign service in the YMCA reached hundreds of students, were both won by unknown Sunday school teachers.

At thirteen years of age Frances Havergal was converted through the influence of her teacher, whose name we do not know. Because she experienced personal salvation this talented girl became a composer whose hymns have inspired hundreds of thousands.

Someone has said, "There is no limit to what you can do if you don't care who gets the credit."

The world may never know our name and our students may not remember our name, but if they remember that we loved them and that we helped point them to Christ, that's all that counts.

Lord, You have promised we shall not be forgotten by You. Let us not worry over the fact that people may not remember us; let's just make sure they don't forget how much You love them. Amen.

47
Little Is Much

"You have been trustworthy in a very small matter" (Luke 19:17).

Horatius Bonar, "the prince of Scottish hymnwriters," once commented,

> A holy life is made up of a multitude of small things. It is the little things of the hour . . . that fill up a life like that of the Apostles Paul or John, or David Brainard. . . . Little words, not eloquent speeches or sermons, little deeds, not miracles or battles; or one great heroic effort of martyrdom. . . . It's the little constant sunbeam, not the lightning."[37]

George William Curtis wrote along this same line, "An engine of one-cat power, running all the time, is more effective than one of forty horsepower standing idle."[38]

And as someone else put it, "It's not our *ability* that counts; it's our *availability*."

It is wonderful to be a person of many talents, to be able to sing, to play instruments, to write well, to paint beautiful drawings. But if no one can count on us to be at our post Sunday after Sunday, what good are these talents?

Love is not a talent. Caring is not a talent. Concern is not a talent. They are gifts from God, free for the asking, and they improve with use. No depreciation here.

Don't lament what you are not. Be what you can. Do what you can. As much as you can. That's all God expects. Remember David and Saul's armor.

Lord, help us to remember that compassion for the multitude shows itself in concern for the individual. Let us be faithful in the job you have given us, whether it be big or small. Amen.

48
The Faithful Shepherd

"If a man owns a hundred sheep, and one of them wanders away, will he not leave the ninety-nine on the hills and go to look for the one that wandered off?" (Matthew 18:12).

A father took his son on his knee and told him the Parable of the Lost Sheep. A shepherd carefully tended his flock of one hundred sheep. One day one sheep wandered away. Even though the shepherd had ninety-nine others, he left his flock to search for the one lost sheep. When he found it, he joyfully put it on his shoulders and carried it home. Then he called his friends and neighbors and said, "Rejoice with me; I have found my lost sheep."

Just as the shepherd faithfully took care of his flock, as teachers we try to tend the "flock" God has given us. Even though we are caring for our students, one may occasionally leave the fold and wander off. When a student is absent several Sundays, let us show our concern for his well-being and try to discover the reason for his absence. As we emulate the Good Shepherd, our students will see the love of Christ through our actions.

Lord, help us to be concerned for every member of our class and to actively follow up those who are absent. Amen.

49
One Day at a Time

"Do not worry about tomorrow, for tomorrow will worry about itself" (Matthew 6:34).

An elderly man in California began cutting trees to construct a log house. A neighbor who knew his purpose and also his age asked him, "Isn't that too large an undertaking for you?"

"It would be," replied the man, "if I looked beyond the chopping of the trees and sawing of logs, and pictured myself laying the foundation and erecting the walls and putting on the roof. Carrying the load all at once would exhaust me. But it isn't much of a job to cut down this little tree, and that's all I have to do right now."[39]

We get discouraged in our task when we look too far ahead. When we're asked to teach a Sunday school class, we say, "Me? Teach a class Sunday after Sunday, month after month?" No wonder we're discouraged. We need to just take it a Sunday at a time.

We can also carry this analogy over to the results. The British statesman Benjamin Disraeli was asked how he bravely went on without seeing results from many of his efforts. He answered, "Have you ever watched a stonecutter at work? He will hammer away at a rock for perhaps 100 times without a crack showing in it. Then at the one hundred first blow, it will split in two. It was not that blow alone which accomplished the result," Disraeli admitted, "but the 100 others that went before it."

One Sunday school lesson, one act of love, one home

visit—added to those before it—may just be the one to crack the shell of that student we thought was so hard.

Lord, help us to take life one day at a time and do our best that day, knowing that eventually we will see the results. Amen.

50
"Take Care of My Sheep"

"Again Jesus said, 'Simon, son of John, do you truly love me?' He answered, 'Yes, Lord; you know that I love you.' Jesus said, 'Take care of my sheep' " (John 21:16).

The One Lost Sheep

We oft hear the plea for trying to keep
   "The lambs of the flock" in the fold,
And well we may; but what of the sheep?
   Shall they be left out in the cold?

It was a sheep, not a lamb, that wandered away,
   In the parable Jesus told,
A grown-up sheep that had gone far astray
   From the ninety and nine in the fold.

Out in the wilderness, out in the cold,
   It was a sheep the Good Shepherd sought;
And back to the flock, safe into the fold,
   It was a sheep the Good Shepherd brought.

And why for the sheep must we earnestly long,

And as earnestly hope and pray?
Because there is danger, if they go wrong,
   They will lead the young lambs away.

For the lambs will follow the sheep, you know,
   Wherever the sheep may stray;
If the sheep go wrong, it will not be long
   Till the lambs are as wrong as they.

And so with the sheep we earnestly plead,
   For the sake of the lambs today.
If the lambs are lost, what a terrible cost
   Some sheep will have to pay![40]

Many of the books for Sunday school workers are written for teachers of children. Teachers of adult classes are often forgotten. It is true, most Christians were converted as a child, and it is important to reach the children before they are lost to the church, but what about reaching the parents? If the children are won and go back to an unchristian home, how long will they last?

Lord, help us who teach the parents to realize they also must be prayed for and called upon, for if they are lost, the lambs may be also. Amen.

51
God's Instrument

"We have this treasure in jars of clay to show that this all-surpassing power is from God and not from us" (2 Corinthians 4:7).

Once, Paganini, "the greatest of all violinists in technical accomplishment,"[41] broke string after string of his violin during a performance. Men had come to hear his greatest sonata, "Napoleon." They hissed as he seemed to destroy all hope for continuing his performance. Then the artist held up his violin: "One string—and Paganini," and on that one string he made the first complete manifestation of his greatness![42]

It is said that Thomas Gainsborough, the "most versatile and original" of the English 18th-century painters[43] longed to be a musician. He bought musical instruments of many kinds and tried to play them. He once heard a great violinist bringing ravishing music from his instrument. Gainsborough was charmed and thrown into transports of admiration. He bought the violin on which the master played so marvelously. He thought that if he had that wonderful instrument that he could play, too. But he soon learned that the music was not in the violin, but was in the master who played it.[44]

Are you discouraged because you have so little strength, no ability you can call your own? Are you dejected because you have no resources? Think, then, what this may mean: one hour, one talent—and God!

One hour each Sunday to teach your students the Word of God and how to apply it to their lives during the week, one talent—yours—completely surrendered to God to be used as He sees fit and where He deems best, and God! The hour without God is wasted; the talent unsurrendered to God is useless. With God, both the hour and the talent will bear fruit.

Lord, help us to remember that we are only the strings of Your instrument. Let us put ourselves wholly at Your service. Amen.

52
The Way

" 'This is the way; walk in it' " (Isaiah 30:21).

An old Chinese philosopher was asked what was the greatest joy he had found in life. "A child," he replied, "going down the road singing after asking me the way."[45]

> An old man, going a lone highway,
> Came at the evening, cold and gray,
> To a chasm, vast and deep and wide,
> Through which was flowing a sullen tide.
> The old man crossed in the twilight dim;
> The sullen stream had no fears for him;
> But he turned when safe on the other side
> And built a bridge to span the tide.
>
> "Old man," said a fellow pilgrim near,
> "You are wasting strength with building here;
> Your journey will end with the ending day,
> You never again must pass this way;
> You have crossed the chasm, deep and wide—
> Why build you the bridge at the eventide?"
>
> The builder lifted his old gray head:
> "Good friend, in the path I have come,"
>   he said,
> "There followeth after me today
> A youth whose feet must pass this way:
> This chasm that has been naught to me
> To that fair-haired youth may a pitfall be.
> He, too, must cross in the twilight dim:

Good friend, I am building the bridge for
   him."[46]

> —Will Allen Dromgoole
> "The Bridge Builder"

Lord, help us to make the way to You plain, never an obstacle course. And where our students need bridges to You, may we build them—or be them. Amen.

Notes

[1] Mrs. Charles E. Cowman, *Springs in the Valley* (Grand Rapids: Zondervan Publishing House, 1939), p. 10.

[2] Hannah Whitall Smith, *The Christian's Secret of a Happy Life* (New York: Grosset and Dunlap, n.d.), p. 145.

[3] Hebert V. Prochnow, *The Speaker's Treasury for Sunday School Teachers* (Boston: W. A. Wilde Co., 1955), p. 21.

[4] B. V. Seals, *Beside the Shepherd's Tent* (Kansas City: Beacon Hill Press, 1956), pp. 41-43. Used by permission.

[5] Robert Troutman, *Better Senior High Teaching* (Kansas City: Beacon Hill Press, 1963), pp. 21, 22. Used by permission.

[6] *Ibid.*

[7] From *Evangelistic Illustrations for Pulpit and Platform* by G. Franklin Allee. Copyright 1961 by G. Franklin Allee.

[8] A. S. London, "An English Criminal," *Youth Evangelism* (Kansas City: Nazarene Publishing House, 1935), p. 31. Used by permission.

[9] Selected from *Our Daily Bread* (Grand Rapids: Radio Bible Class), January 27, 1982. Used by permission.

[10] John Donne, *Devotions Upon Emergent Occasions.*

[11] Allee, *Evangelistic Illustrations for Pulpit and Platform,* p. 50.

[12] Betty Barnett Griffith, *The Challenge of Caravan* (Kansas City: Nazarene Publishing House, 1969), pp. 48, 49. Used by permission.

[13] Adapted from a list in "Essentials of Leadership," by Dr. H. S. Horn of Columbia University.

[14] Adapted from Mary E. Latham, *Teacher, You Are an Evan-*

gelist (Kansas City: Beacon Hill Press, 1963). Used by permission.

[15]Adapted from A. C. Archer, *Notions, Nuggets, Bumpers, Breakers* (Portland, OR: A. C. Archer, 1935), pp. 58, 59.

[16]Allee, *Evangelistic Illustrations for Pulpit and Platform,* p. 160.

[17]Andrew Murray, *With Christ in the School of Prayer* (Old Tappan, NJ: Fleming H. Revell Co., 1895).

[18]Allee, *Evangelistic Illustrations for Pulpit and Platform,* p. 41.

[19]Leonard Bolton, *China Call* (Springfield, MO: Gospel Publishing House, 1984), p. 66.

[20]Allee, *Evangelistic Illustrations for Pulpit and Platform,* p. 283.

[21]Excerpt from *Lessons From Life* by Robert I. Kahn. Copyright © 1963 by Robert I. Kahn. Reprinted by permission of Doubleday & Company, Inc.

[22]Adapted from Allee, *Evangelistic Illustrations for Pulpit and Platform,* p. 89.

[23]Selected from *Our Daily Bread,* December 4, 1981. Used by permission.

[24]John Oxenham, "Bees in Amber" (American Tract Society, 1913).

[25]Selected from *Our Daily Bread,* February 7, 1982. Used by permission.

[26]From Leader's Guide to *Who's First?* by Emily Moore. (Kansas City: Beacon Hill Press, 1976.) Used by permission.

[27]Cowman, *Springs in the Valley,* p. 10.

[28]*The Secret Place* (Valley Forge, PA: American Baptist Churches), January 29, 1982.

[29]Selected from *Our Daily Bread,* February 19, 1982. Used by permission.

[30]D. L. Moody, *Easy to Live With.*

[31]Prochnow, *The Speaker's Treasury for Sunday School Teachers,* p. 37.

[32]Hazel A. Lewis, *Planning for Children in Your Church* (St. Louis: Bethany Press, 1947), p. 73.

[33] Prochnow, *The Speaker's Treasury for Sunday School Teachers,* p. 14.

[34] *Ibid.,* p. 49.

[35] A. S. London, *Youth Evangelism,* p. 45. Used by permission.

[36] Prochnow, *The Speaker's Treasury for Sunday School Teachers,* p. 47.

[37] Selected from *Our Daily Bread,* December 8, 1981. Used by permission.

[38] Allee, *Evangelistic Illustrations for Pulpit and Platform,* p. 115.

[39] Selected from *Our Daily Bread,* December 1, 1981. Used by permission.

[40] Latham, *Teacher, You Are an Evangelist.* Used by permission.

[41] *The New College Encyclopedia of Music,* 1960 ed., s.v. "Paganini."

[42] Cowman, *Springs in the Valley,* p. 114.

[43] *Encyclopedia Britannica,* 1973 ed., s.v. "Gainsborough."

[44] Cowman, *Springs in the Valley,* p. 114.

[45] Prochnow, *The Speaker's Teasury for Sunday School Teachers.*

[46] Will Allen Dromgoole "The Bridge Builder," *Masterpieces of Religious Verse* (Nashville, TN: Broadman Press, n.d.), #1083.